"*The Little Book of Me* is not that little, full as it is with the astute observations, wit, poignancy, and insight of the me in its title. Patricia Lawson lets us spy on a child who stars in a life she has made up; she reminds us of the self-absorption of adolescence so 'bent on losing . . . innocence' that others become merely backgrounds in their picture. She pulls the blinds wide open on midlife and marriage when the bride, who had once 'momentarily taken over the game' becomes she who 'keels the pots' while the rest of the family watches the game. Inevitably, old age opens its 'unwelcome portal' through which none of us runs 'thin as a thistle.' But life is way more than its arc. There are travels with heavy-drinking friends, and cats who may become so numerous as to be a 'carpet of cats' moving across the back yard. From moments of intense pique to a snowy afternoon so silent that 'If God spoke, he would sound like Edward R. Murrow,' this collection is a trip I'm so glad I took. I think you will love it, too."

-Eve Ott, *Album from the Silent Generation*

"Wry, witty, and often laugh-out-loud funny, Pat Lawson thoroughly entertains in this journey through childhood, adolescence, marriage, adulthood, aging, gardening, travel abroad, neighborhood life, and cats—a narrative of life. Though readers may chuckle reading these poems, throughout is an underlying current of acute observation and wisdom, and *The Little Book of Me,* becomes the little book of we as readers find both the personal and the universal."

-Maryfrances Wagner, *The Immigrants' New Camera*

"Pat Lawson's poetry draws the reader in and holds the reader in thrall. She has an astonishing gift for language, and *The Little Book of Me* proves it. Her subjects run the gambit from cats and foreign travel to weeds and weddings. Along the way, we see outstanding imagery, original and appropriate word choices. Describing bugs flying around a light, she says 'small, green insects flitted and crisped.' Never is a poem obscure. Her work exudes accessibility. Whatever the topic, she captures its essence, The reader enters 'Grandmother's Kitchen,' watches as young children at a wedding reception 'take to the floor,' learns about her past boyfriends through writing that is evocative and fresh. This is a book to finish at one sitting, a compelling book. Not all is serious here. Just when you think you know where the poem is going, she tosses in a humorous curve, sardonic and otherwise. This is a brilliant collection in which Lawson has captured 'the big wide waters of the world," hers and ours.'"

-R. Nikolas Macioci, author of *Why Dance?* and *Dark Guitar*

"Put on your bib and dig in. Discover yourself and fill your belly with Patricia Lawson's *The Little Book of Me*. This impeccably-crafted, strongly-narrative collection focuses on ten facets of life and create a delightful, lavish table. Her work sizzles, resonates, permeates, sticks to your bones. Her poetry toasts you. It says, "Welcome to your place at the feast."

-Sandra Feen, *Fragile Capacities: School Poems*

The Little Book of Me

Poems by Patricia Lawson

Kansas City   Missouri

Spartan Press
Kansas City, Missouri
spartanpress.com

Copyright © Patricia Lawson, 2021
First Edition: 1 3 5 7 9 10 8 6 4 2
ISBN: 978-1-952411-41-0
LCCN: 2020952987

Author photo: Chris Mullins
All rights reserved. No part of this publication may be reproduced or transmitted in any form or by any means, electronic or mechanical, including photocopying, recording, or by info retrieval system, without prior written permission from the author.

The author would like to thank Spartan Press and editor Jason Ryberg for accepting and publishing this book and the following publications where these poems first appeared:

The Shining Years: Poems About Aging: "Abandoned,"

The Same: "Duo," "Garden Speaker," "Mullein," "Spending," "Greasy Joan," "Midwinter Light," "Backdrop," "Brushes with Fame," "Kansas City Bower," "Midas," "Someday You May Find Yourself at MacDonald's," "The Cat," "Cat's Dream," "Willy Nilly," "Table Rock Lake, November 8, 2006"

Thorny Locust: "Twenty-one Countries on My Street," "Rock Pigeons"

I-70 Review: "Foreigners have such a Je Ne Sais Quoi"

Why We Love Our Cats and Dogs (Unholy Day Press, co-authored with Philip Miller): "Willy Nilly" and "The Black Cat" (as "Black Cat"),

Coal City Review: "Last View?"

The Kansas City Star: "Tweak"

River King Poetry Supplement: "At the All-Day Meeting"

Curating Home: A Kansas City Poetry Anthology: "The Little Creek"

TABLE OF CONTENTS

Kansas City Bower / 1

Star / 2

Spending / 3

Carl / 4

Grandmother's Kitchen / 5

To the Drugstore / 7

Boyfriends / 8

Wedding Day / 10

Wedding Dancers / 13

Greasy Joan / 14

Brushes with Fame / 16

Midas / 18

In the Community College Learning Center / 19

Someday You May Find Yourself at MacDonald's / 20

Sluggish on the Sofa / 22

Christmas Day / 25

The Months Slip By / 29

Old Pets / 30

Auld Pets / 31

I Went to My Granddaughter's Book Club / 32

Abandoned / 34

Vultures / 36

Last View? / 37

Twenty-one Countries on My Street / 41

In My Neighborhood / 42

Mid-winter Light / 43

April Evening in Kansas City / 44

Rock Pigeons / 45

Country Picnic / 49

June / 50

Shhhhhh / 51

Table Rock Lake, November 6, 2006 / 52

Vertigo / 53

Past Gardens / 57

Garden in a Small Town in Oklahoma / 58

Garden Speaker / 59

Mullein / 60

The Dismal Garden / 61

In the Garden with Thousands of Little Friends / 62

Backdrop / 67

Foreigners Have Such a *Je Ne Sai Quoi* / 68

Visiting My Brother in Hungary, 1978 / 69

Foreign Tongues / 70

With My Heavy-Drinking Friends in Europe / 71

Out for a Walk / 73

Willy Nilly / 77

The Black Cat / 78

Snow Scene with Cats / 79

The House Cat Vents / 80

Cat People / 81

At the All-Day Meeting / 85

Cross Patch / 87

Damn Cross / 88

Christmas Shopping / 90

Tweak / 92

Without Fear of Plummeting / 95

Contemplatives / 96

MRI / 97

Recycled / 98

Duo / 99

It Was Green / 100

The Little Creek / 101

For The Collaborators and The Diversifiers:

Kathy Allen, Janice Atkins, Phyllis Becker, James Benger,
Carl Bettis, Anne Calvert, Conci Denniston, Ethan Denniston,
Nancy Eldredge, Ida Fogle, Vicki Garton, Beth Gulley,
Z. Hall, Jim Jandt, Silvia Kofler, Elaine Lally, Phil Miller,
Colleen Maynard, Dolores Miller, Patricia Miller, Eve Ott,
Michelle Pond, Randy Ratliff, Andres Rodriguéz,
Rhiannon Ross, Mark Schroer, Gib Shell, Gloria Vando

For my original little family—my parents, Carl and Sylvia
Hoff; sister, Audrie Seeley, shown next to my mother on the
back cover; brother, Dudley Hoff, the likely photographer;
cousins, Jean Nylund, Mary Ann Potter (see front cover.
Right to left are Audrie, Jeannie, me, Mary Ann); cousin,
John Bussard; my aunt and uncle, Mary Elizabeth and
Louis Bussard.

I celebrate myself, and sing myself.

-Walt Whitman

Young Me

How I once loved Kenny S. and Little Whatever . . .

Kansas City Bower

When I was five, below our house
a concrete culvert made a course
through which a city sewer ran,
channeling nature while above
Nature had its way, though it (or she)
by accident had formed a bower.
I didn't know then what *bower* meant
or *thicket,* my mother's word
for the thick cave of shrubs
I might slip into and lose myself,
and since I couldn't see inside
and couldn't name what might be there—
elf or *snake* or *crawly thing*—
that bower (or thicket) frightened me.
What it needed was a bower bird,
coming, going, "decorating,"
or at the very least a crow,
carrying in a marble, coin,
ring, trinket, bit of glass,
some small human artifact.

Star

She is a star in a play she's made up,
a musical she enters wearing
a blue slip and sheer white curtain.

She climbs to the top of a slope,
strolls downhill or runs pell-mell
down the path she's trampled
through her mother's vinca.
Jacks watch from their pulpits
as she sings of her "Alice-blue gown,"
using nonsense words
to fill up the stanzas.

Or she sits on the swing in the back yard,
sailing above the vines and weeds,
beneath the tops of oaks
for an audience of squirrels,
who throw acorns at her feet.

She swings so long she misses Baby Snooks,
but sometimes she is Snooks
and sometimes the Lone Ranger.

Stage left is a sidewalk and apartment building.
Uphill and upstage center is the back
of a bigger house on a nicer street.
Stage right, another house like hers.
Downstage is a small brown house
with her parents inside on the couch,
watching the little Zenith.

Spending

My parents taught us money-saving ways.
We learned to shrink down in our shoes
and look eleven at all those entrances
where twelve-year-olds had to pay a quarter more,
and how to make a long-distance call
and say "She's not home" for "all is well."

My brother, their disciple, now buys generic.
Saturdays his family heads for the park.
My sister, the lost child, marrying into a tribe
of shoppers, converted, and doesn't bat an eye
for forking over lots of dough for lots of stuff.
She'll buy your meal, your drinks, your ticket.

I love her generosity, and sometimes
I too can work myself up for a grand gesture,
like the satellite dish for my in-laws,
which didn't work and which they didn't want.
But I can't quit looking over my shoulder.

It's not that I'm a piker.
It's just each spent sum makes a little shade
that sits with us on the new patio chairs,
comes in with the dog through the new doggy door,
hangs around with the family in the hot tub
we bought for a song at the wholesale club.

Carl

On trips to the Ozarks in the station wagon
with three whiny kids in the back
and a wife, who made the plans, up front,
he'd stop at a liquor store,
buy a little bourbon
to steady his nerves.
At the cabin he'd withdraw,
leaving the kids with their mother,
emerging later to face
the cold river, the mosquitoes, the stinking bait.
At night, after supper, he'd have another.
Outside, the kids, his own and others,
spat watermelon seeds.
Some fallen child was wailing,
his wife berating.
Inside the musty cabin
the fan clattered and droned.
The water smelled of sulfur.
The darting mosquitoes whined
as he sat reading by the light
around which small, green insects
flitted and crisped.
But after midnight, when the exhausted children slept,
and his wife snored softly beside him,
he felt the beginnings of coolness.
Insect sounds merged into a single tone.
Then he felt his nerves restoring.
He stretched his toes against the cotton sheet.

Grandmother's Kitchen

The cupboards were neatly stacked:
Moderntone dishes in pastelish blue,
pink, green, and citrus yellow.
Sitting at her tiny kitchen table
with the bowl of waxed fruit,
I'd study the cherries on the patterned wall
as she cooked—just for me now,
my grandfather dead several years.
She'd open the usual can of grapefruit,
place the arched bacon on my plate,
whistling all the while she cooked,
"Mairzy Doats" or "Old Susannah"
without her old enthusiasm.

When I was twenty and in college,
but still my grandmother's girl,
I saw the floor had grown greasy,
and there were roaches.
She seldom whistled any more
and barely cooked.
And soon she became an emaciated woman
making guttural sounds in a bed.

I still see her in the prim kitchen,
making her careful ministrations,
taking great pains with a waffle,
see the pastel plate before me.

Now I whistle too,
mostly to entertain my grandson,
who stares at me
as if I've turned into a bird.

To the Drugstore

On the way to the drugstore, in those days,
Mary Beth took me under her wing,
shared her thoughts on popularity:
Rah-rah boys and *tee-hee girls.*
She bleached her hair like Kim Novak's,
sang "I Want To Be Evil" by Eartha Kitt,
told me all her family's failings,
sister's affair with a married guy.
At the drugstore we'd gossip
as we drank our lemon Cokes
and whispered that the druggist
must be an alcoholic,
or why the red nose?
And why so standoffish?
We might have said he was *solemn,*
but it wasn't in our vocabulary.
Neither was *desolate.*
We were only bent on losing our innocence,
having all revealed,
and in the background,
Mr. Polsky brooded.

Boyfriends

How I once loved Kenny S and Little Whatever
his last name was—I can't remember.
(His big brother was cute too, Big Whatever.)
Neither Kenny nor Little
liked me much—I was rather pitiful,
but I adored them,
especially Little with his soulful eyes;
he had possibilities
unearthed by me,
his devotee.
There was A, a football player,
sort of average and squarish,
sort of dim.
(Did he drop me?
Or I, him?)
And J with the dreadful acne.
I couldn't get beyond his looks.
I was shallow
if you want to know.
But later I fell for another boy
with a bad complexion,
loved him to distraction.
He was so angelic and pale
and disdainful.
And later came P,
who loved me most—

dumb as a post,
and another A,
who squeezed me in forbidden places.
I smacked him on the face,
which you were supposed to do
in '62.
He was very rich,
but his ears stuck out,
giving me the miseries.
Oh, how Love disappointed me.

Wedding Day

Why is the wedding day the "bride's day"?
It is. Photographs prove it.
My mother, looking as if she could wow the whole world.
My daughter, in her huge, white princess gown,
like a Miss America winner, no longer humble or coy.
And me, fat-faced and smug, cutting the cake.
The husbands are always shown off center—
sickly, sardonic, weary, bemused.
You would think it would be the opposite.
The men would all be on thrones
instead of looking like foot soldiers.
But no, the brides are happy, happy women,
like quiz-show contestants,
who have learned the crazy rules
and, using them to advantage,
have momentarily taken over the game.

Mid-life Me

*What you all will be is
fodder for a background shot
in some Chevy Chase movie . . .*

Wedding Dancers

Who wins our hearts at weddings?
Not the bride or groom or the sad-faced father,
not the tipsy woman making sloppy passes.
It's the toddlers on the dance floor.
While others are gossiping
or practicing wedding politics,
ignoring the music or using it to advantage,
they take to the floor like anarchists,
little heedless red-faced dancers,
high on cake and free of coercion.
One in pink barrettes does a twist in waltz time.
Another with untucked shirt
marches in a square he has imagined.
A chunky red-haired girl
pulls off her purple ribbons
and twirls them about herself.
One circles the bride; one circles a pole.
Two hold hands and spin until they drop.
They make up the dances to suit themselves
while we sit stolidly in our chairs
as if in church or chamber.
They are our representatives.

Greasy Joan

When roasted crabs hiss in the bowl,
Then nightly sings the string owl,
                Tu-who:
Tu-whit, tu-who! A merry note!
While Greasy Joan doth keel the pot.

          -William Shakespeare

As cold gains a tighter grip,
and meals grow heartier,
Joan is in the kitchen
where she stews, bastes, and broils,
works up a sweat,
sets the feast on the table,
hops up to fetch the butter.
"More sauce!" "Too much pepper!"
"Tu-whit, to-who," the family's ringing note.
"Dessert time and better be quick."
"Kickoff time approacheth."
She clears the table, rinses dishes.
Her hands and arms grow scummy
as the kitchen sink, a greasy orange.
Her teeth are set on edge
as she scrapes knuckle bones into the trash
and garbage down the sink,
fends off the dogs,
clears the countertop of cats
while inside the living room
the family cheer or boo the plays,
some enthroned on the couch,
menials crouching on the floor.

Children whine. Their noses drip.
And in the kitchen Greasy Joan
keels the pots, hearkens to the owl's cry.

Brushes with Fame

1.
It's 6 a.m. I'm sitting on a bench
near Central Park drinking coffee,
having just come in on the red-eye from KC,
and this man sits down and says,
"Lady, if you sit here awhile,
you'll see Lauren Bacall walk her dog."
So I sit and sit, but Lauren doesn't show.
But I see this gray-haired man
who's in lots of commercials.
He plays a jovial exterminator.
You'd know him if you saw him.

2,
I might be six degrees of separation
from Nelson Mandela or any Kennedy,
but I'm only four from Sting.
I know a gal whose brother's
girlfriend coached Sting in yoga.
And Drew Carey—only three.
My hairdresser met his nephew,
said the nephew was pretty cool.
And a mere two from Harry Truman,
who was Dad's defender
when Dad drove drunk.

3.

And the people I've known!
A runner up for Miss Missouri,
a kid almost electrocuted entering a metal shed,
a double-jointed guy who liked to sit
with one leg wrapped about his neck,
and a very old woman, friend of my mother,
who appeared on "I've Got a Secret."
When the panel couldn't guess,
she took off her turban and let fall,
her long, thin hair,
and then she stood on it.

Midas

Dr. Pete Petrakis,
the eminent plastic surgeon,
can make any woman golden
through skilled application
of Juvaderm or micro-dermabrasion.
Sometimes there's a bit of suffering
before a glow is attained.
In the meantime, healing is enhanced
in the doctor's office by soothing music
that suggests the pipes of Pan,
and the tinkling of the fountain
in the marble entranceway,
inset with golden flecks.
One feels a very goddess
when one passes through the door.
One feels burnished,
not unlike the Kohler faucets,
as light surrounds one in
a flattering golden pink,
and the dark tiles give off
a thousand gilded winks.

In the Community College Learning Center

Every weekday at eleven, one duo at a time,
I'd sit side by side with a student,
checking to see if he or she had shifted verbs,
spliced with commas, fused sentences,
whether participles dangled or clung.
Were the antecedents clear?
Had parallel elements jumped the track?

What became of Joel, the red-haired guy,
who never caught on, though we labored long?
Or the quiet brown-haired girl,
pregnant before her two-young marriage
and wedding feast at the Forum Cafeteria?
The timid, agreeable Mrs. R,
who couldn't recognize
a fragment if it flew at her?

In the Learning Center,
how we all bore down,
clenching our ballpoints.

Someday You May Find Yourself at MacDonald's

. . . en route somewhere
with your extended family,
all of you milling about
in, maybe, baseball caps
or identical tee-shirts:
Henshaw Family Reunion:
August 12-13, 2000
Des Moines, Iowa.
And you will find yourself
as run-of-the-mill
as anyone's family.
Beside you, Aunt Charlotte,
as short and stout and dyed
as anybody's aunt.
And your cousin's spindly boys—
as unpromising as many a boy
you'd find in fast food joints.
And the toddlers will be food-stained,
even some of the adults.
And as for you!
In the restroom light
(except for the shirt)
you'll look no different
from all the fluorescent-lit, road-tired women
you've seen in other way stations.
And what you all will be is
fodder for a background shot

in some Chevy Chase movie
where the camera pans
the campy shirts, the weary faces,
the scrawny kid with glasses and buck teeth,
just like you at eleven.
Little snapshots of Americana.
You've seen it all before.

Sluggish on the Sofa

                . . . sated from the lasagna,
I stare at the starlings
            settling in trees,
Like black spots or specks,
            sparrows' droppings,
Or an old crumbled croissant
            cast far afield.
And now they fly furious
            in forms like linguine,
Now bloom and burgeon
            in billowing masses,
Or like blades of a blender,
            burring and purring,
And I yearn for the years
            of my youth, which have fled
When thin as a thistle,
            I ran thoughtless and coltish
Or went muddled and mulish
            if my mood so decreed,
For often I was obstinate
            like an oblivious tortoise
Bearing its bounty,
            mayhap a bright beetle
In its jammed-tight jaws
            its job to plod down
Some hellish highway
            where hurtling trucks plow
As in the book by Steinbeck . . .

Oh, fudge! I forget!
>	I ran fast as a deer,

Always passing on pasta,
>	preferring Spam,

Never bothering with bread,
>	which I bought for the pigeons,

Always omnipresent,
>	but obviously unorganized.

Their schemes unfortunately followed,
>	feckless creatures.

The cocks went Hitchcockian.
>	We couldn't believe it.

And we overheard with horror
>	their heartless conniving,

Their plucking and plotting . . .
>	But the pigeons are background.

What I meant to mention
>	is my once great metabolism,

Then gradually, gradually as
>	rock gives way to water,

Bad carbs crept in
>	corrupting our diets.

(Not from tamale carts,
>	which taught us diversity.)

I blame Campbell's creations,
>	casseroles with cream soup,

Chef Boyardee's benisons
>	I brought into the house,

Especially Spaghettios.
>
> Never sparing, I ate them,

And Hamburger Helper
>
> seemed to hatch in the cupboard.

Glycemic glutton,
>
> I was gleeful and innocent.

Craver of cannelloni,
>
> I needed my comforts.

All this sapped my strength.
>
> Now I snooze on the sofa.

Where is yesterday's youth?
>
> Yes, gone with the snow.

Christmas Day

With an hour or two to kill, alone,
I stare at photos of the dead—
first the partly dead,
myself and my husband in our youth,
our children in their infancy.
Then the totally dead—
father-in-law in overalls
and western hat, hands at his sides,
and in the upper right corner
part of the finger of my mother-in-law,
who died a year ago,
and a picture of my mother as flapper,
though this would be her centennial,
and at my father, debonair, bright-eyed,
with cigarette in hand,
looking so young and smart,
so assured of the future.

Old Me

Good-bye old friends, deserters.

The Months Slip By

            fast and faster.
Christmas sneaks up on you.
Close behind comes Valentine's Day,
Easter, your May birthday. Thanksgiving
and the dark season follows so fast
it seems summer must have been a figment.
Someone talks of *evanescence* in
a tone that says it's something rare,
but it's in the very air in which
friends, family, celebrities, the guy down the street
are here, passing, gone. Things too
sail past, like projectiles—
houses, cars, your books, eyeglasses,
wine glasses (how many smashed?).
And those old clothes you wear—
it seems you bought them yesterday, yet they've
hung in the closet for years. The granddaughter,
who once was two, is suddenly twelve,
and now the things that plague your friends
fill up their calls, so you can barely
mention your old dog, your worn shoes,
your creaking knees. The rout is on,
and all you can do is stand and stare.

Old Pets

I've a vintage cat and a vintage dog.
The dog has bad breath and a dumbstruck look.
All winter he lies on his side
in the middle of the rug
and wheezes a soft lament.
The cat is thin, with a pinched mug.
Her hair sticks up; her bones stick out.
She spends her days beneath a quilt,
appears suddenly, like a wraith,
to stare at me with her green-gold eyes.
My days are spent with these old pets.
We hear the wind blow through the trees,
the cars whiz by the house.
It's warm inside by the old TV,
and nothing but cold without.

Auld Pets

("Scottish" version—with apologies to Robert Burns)

I've an auld cat and an auld dog.
The dog has bad breath and a dumbstruck look.
A' winter he lies on his side
in the middle of the rug
and wheezes a soft lament.
The cat is thin with a pinched gob.
Her hair sticks up; her bones stick oot.
She spends her days beneath a quilt,
appears suddenly like a wraith
to staur at me with her green-gaold een.
My days are spent with these auld pets.
We hear the wind braw through the trees,
the cars whiz by the hoose.
It's warm inside by the auld TV
and naught but cauld wi'oot.

I Went to My Granddaughter's Book Club

. . . went inside and sat down with her
and other eight- and nine-year-olds
in a circle of wooden chairs,
prepared to discuss *Charlotte's Web.*

A little girl said she loved Wilbur and Charlotte most.
"Oh, so do I," I said, "especially their catalogues—
Charlotte's list of insects, the events of Wilbur's day.
White was a master of the catalogue."

A boy said, "Templeton's really mean."
"Mean, yes," I said, "but not a flat character.
Rat-like, yes, but a multi-leveled picaro,
the Sancho Panza to Wilbur's Quixote.

"Agreed?" I beamed at everyone.
What an insight. Maybe even publishable.
They stared down at their tennies.
The discussion leader too.

Obviously, they held dissenting views.
"Maybe you think Wilbur's the Sancho figure.
But he's naïve, oblivious to his destiny as bacon.
Therefore, he's Quixote, *n'est pas?*"

Then it dawned on me.
These children were themselves naïve.
I smacked my forehead—"What an idiot!" I said,
giving it the French pronunciation—for humor's sake.

No one responded but a boy named Michele,
who gave his own small head an imitative smack.
"You are indeed an idiot," he said and grinned.
Brilliant child. We bonded instantly.

Abandoned

I've noticed aspects, specters, of me
heading for the door.
It all began some time in my middle period
when I lost my 20-20 vision, followed
by my hearing, once so keen I could put
my ear to the ground and hear horses' hooves.

Then my luxuriant hair waxed,
waned, and wandered off.
My teeth uprooted themselves
or were forcibly uprooted.
Luckily, my sturdy-soldier teeth remain,
pillars for the bridge I hope to build one day.

Later, my once keen memory, which kept tabs
on birthdays, grudges, debts,
rode off, like Shane, into the sunset.
A dull creature with vague thoughts moved in,
whose name I can't remember—
Carol or Cheryl or Beryl or something.

Goodbye old friends, deserters.
Farewell, adieu. You are sorely missed,
but had you turned and looked back,
you would have seen me,
the elemental me, still hanging around,

kind of resembling The Blob, but smaller,
not so red and slimy, much less threatening,
with a bit more form—
two legs for wearing faded jeans,
a hand for waving bye-bye.

Vultures

(after Elizabeth Bishop)

The leaves are an early green,
the redbud studded with pink
and down below, the stink

of something rotting draws these birds,
who wheel around the something as the planets turn
around the star that holds our world.

We watch in fascination
the varying degrees of their orbital inclination.
Something below awaits purification.

Or maybe we recall Faulkner's Bundrens
who have the effrontery
to take their mother's body cross country.

Part of us wants to shut its eyes,
yet we watch as one and then another drops from the skies
below the canopy to where the hidden carcass lies.

Watching then dip and soar,
we are given an unwelcome portal,
through which we can't evade that we are mortal.

Last View?

From the window of the ambulance making its run,
passing a winter scene—iron bridge,
black starlings dipping and rising
against a rose-gray sky?

Or a sky bright as a beach ball,
leaves on a maple drooping,
flash of yellow from a goldfinch?

Or at home, from a bed,
sharp image in the doorway.
Your pastor in aqua shirtsleeves?

Or blurry—of sister? Friend?
Aunt, dead ten years?
Anyway, someone in peachy beige
with pale skin and sandy hair.

Or from below, staring up
at the ring of people staring down?

An on-your-side perspective?
Separated by chainlink diamonds,
from a yard with chickens
(or pigeons) pecking at grit?

From your belly,
a view from beneath the lowest board
of a cedar fence, glimpse
of grassy stubble, gravel,

and beyond the stubble,
possibly some sort of court,
ankles and tennis shoes,
soles like wings?

Me, Urbanite

. . . the Kaw River has turned into the Tiber.

Twenty-one Countries on My Street

The country of invisible people,
El pais en el modo de México, with tile and folk art,
The country where people are brave in their illness,
The country of the cheerful, who smile and volunteer,
The country of sky-blue houses encircled by countries whose citizens prefer earth tones,
Eceentrica, where a man can grow wild flowers or weeds if he wishes,
Birdlandia, whose citizens have the names of birds, and the figures of birds adorn their houses,
The country whose people make statements with tulips,
The country of people with family values and cars that belch smoke,
The country where people preach kindness but practice coldness,
El pais del miserables, whose houses sink into the ground,
A country run by cats, who parade in the street,
The country of sharp-dressed old white people who frequent taverns,
The country of garrulous black folks,
The country of old German widows,
The country of young men who have gone off to war,
The country of people in non-military uniforms, who still look important,
The country of blonde policemen,
El pais de panaderos*
El pais de enamorados.**
This is our little world.

bakers
**lovers*

In My Neighborhood

    there is the house with wide-set windows
that has an innocent, startled look
though there's not much to startle at.
Is it amazed that this October
is so unseasonably cool?
That the robins left so early?
That two old men grew sick and died?
Perhaps the house remembers
their faces, their poor physiques,
one hobbling, the other struggling
with his appendage of oxygen.
Other houses keep their own counsel,
expressionless houses
with drawn blinds and closed doors,
eyes shuttered in sleep,
except for the one with the curious, goofy look
with its two windows upstairs
and the divided window below that
looks like the teeth of a big rabbit,
Harvey maybe, or Bugs Bunny,
asking the lone walker, cat, or dog,
"What's up, Doc? Why so solemn?"

Mid-winter Light

There's a certain slant of light
Winter Afternoons—
That oppresses, like the Heft
Of Cathedral Tunes...

   -Emily Dickinson

In mid-winter, the light is stern,
and everything in the cityscape denuded
as if God intends a lesson in starkness.
He makes each rusting piece of metal,
each oil-stained sidewalk, each sagging porch apparent.
In the cold clear light in the inner city,
even in the suburbs
every imperfection stands out.
Even at the rich man's mansion,
see how rough the brick, how brash the circle drive.
Up on the second floor, outside a bedroom,
a shutter dangles.
Today a few cars are passing on my street,
but there is no camaraderie,
nowhere voices traveling back and forth between
the houses, which all seem made of tin.
Each house, rich and poor,
stands in its *slant of light*
miserable and cold.
And the occupants? Where are they?
Maybe gone to the tropics
where life glides through a thick forest
bathed in warm-green light.

April Evening in Kansas City

A trick of lighting, thanks to the sun
has turned one skyscraper molten gold.
The windows gleam and pulse like brass.
Buildings on a lower level glow red-gold
like the buildings you'd find in Rome
where, as the light withdraws,
the buildings hold warm undertones
of rose, peach, umber, and sienna
in contrast with the darkening sky,
and it seems for the moment
the Kaw River has turned into the Tiber.

Rock Pigeons

Hundreds sit side by side,
not on a bluff but a narrow metal ledge
at the side of the overpass I pass under,
like ball players on a long bench

or bluish-gray keys in a giant marimba
about to be struck by a Looney Toons giant,
each bird rising to gurgle its *coo-cuh-ruh-cuh-ruh-coo*

or like Hungarian communists in the seventies,
who allowed small deviations,
rusty red on one bird,
gray and black on another,
yet still meeting party standards,
all facing south,

in camouflage against the gunmetal green,
overlooking freight cars in the yard below
with its plentiful supply of grain,
their nests tucked under the overpass,

oblivious to their bad reputations
as rats in need of poisoning.
No one, except an eccentric, feeds pigeons,
even at St. Marks in Venice
where they wander and warble among the tourists,
are photographed and shoved aside.

Me in the Country

". . . oh, the quiet, the dismal, awful quiet."

Country Picnic

Always in late April or Early May, my aunt and uncle
would have a picnic for us in the "timber,"
as they called it, making the little patch of woods
sound far away from their small Missouri farm.
Two carloads of kids and tired adults
would drive over pasture to the woods
through which ran a creek you crossed on stones.
On the bank the grass grew greener than the earliest love,
the youngest chick or child, in thick green clumps,
like ripples over rocks it spread through the woods,
an almost unbroken green, except for the darker tree line
and patches of wild violets, and here and there
the sodden earth or splattered cow pads
we'd stumble over in our wild runs
as we chased each other, screaming through the trees
or stirred up the creek with sticks,
trying to spear fish though we only saw minnows.
We thought the dark creek deeper than they said.

Meanwhile the grownups stretched out
on bumpy blankets spread over those clumps of grass.
After a while, our shrieks grew fainter, and their limbs relaxed.
My mother's foot outstretched to touch my father's.
My pretty, yellow-haired aunt,
away from her wearying chores,
would open a thermos, pour everyone's coffee,
and smile at nothing in particular.
My hard-boiled uncle, no longer staring out the window
at his muddy lot, would watch his smoke drift
among the trees and hang like fog in the air.

June

It's high old summer, the trees fully leaved,
the grass still pushing up fast,
the days soft and a bit too warm,
the grass now yellower green.
We settle into summer's virtues—
softness, ease, a southern way of living.
We are summer's poster children,
sipping our beers and iced teas, swaying in hammocks,
sitting on the deck with feet propped up.
In the back of our minds are the dog days yet to come
when we will need to steel ourselves.
But now, like the Wicked Witch of the West,
we are melting, melting, and nothing can help it.

Shhhhhh

Oh, the quiet, oh the quiet,
the dismal, awful quiet.
I am sitting in the Ozarks
on a green hill, listening to . . .
well, nothing really,
nothing but the quiet.
Now and then a crow caws
or far away a boat thrums,
but mostly it is quiet, quiet, quiet.
I am longing for the city
where from time to time one hears
a jackhammer or a yowling cat.
Here one longs to have a bee buzz by,
just to break the creepy quiet.
I sit watching the leaves move,
but they don't even make a rustle.
So I have to think my Own Thoughts.
But my Own Thoughts are
so dismal and so quiet.

Table Rock Lake, November 6, 2006

Right now, which is 7 a.m., the lake is breathtakingly
    beautiful.
For instance, the sun has made a huge, diaphanous shape
    on its surface,
something like a funnel or pyramid with the point towards me.
Suffice it to say, the lake is large and it sparkles.
Add to that, the surrounding hills shrouded in mists,
which, by the way, obscure the protruding hotel,
The Chateau on the Lake, whose builders had no thought
for the people across the lake, who have to look at it
when it isn't shrouded. But now it is shrouded.
Also, the hills are fairly dark, though up close
there are coppers and bronzes, for it is autumn.
But, overall, they are various colors that add up to dark.
In short, at present, the lake is 100% beautiful,
the view like a Japanese mountain scene.
And though this is southern Missouri, where irony
is heaped upon irony, one could use phrases like
Gift of God or *Nature's Glory*,
depending on one's perspective.

Vertigo

I am in the Ozark Mountains
in a condo named *Tree of Heaven*.
Here it's a Dr. Seussian world
of precarious perches
where birds timidly approach
the suspended, swaying feeder.
Perhaps it will fall and kill someone,
or the beams will give, and I'll fall through.
Oh, the level lake is tranquil,
but from above it seems ready
to collapse in upon itself.
Or become unmoored, like a tourist
who leaves his perfectly good, old wife
standing by the car,
and, wandering to the very edge
of the Majestic Outlook,
feels the gravel slide beneath his feet.

Gardener Me

. . . his garden is given over to oddities.

Past Gardens

Maybe a long time ago you did something extraordinary.
Perhaps, as a child, you made a garden in the back yard.
One year, things grew; another, they didn't.
And later you dreamed of those gardens, their successes
    and failures.
One year you had tomatoes; another, just vines.
One year you even had carnations, or was it petunias?
One year, very little, only a few scraggly blossoms.
But another—did it happen or not—you had the finest
    roses,
a deep, deep pink against dark, waxy leaves.
They must have grown in spite of the shade,
amazing everyone who came into the yard.
Sometimes just one person came, your old grandmother
    perhaps.
Other times groups of neighbors came to admire
your wonderful work. But finally, as you remember,
something much more ordinary occurred—and
    persisted.
The grass came back, but mostly weeds took over.
The roses (or marigolds) failed to thrive.
But maybe dandelions bloomed—or plantain weed
in a mass of glossy green. Disappointing,
but beautiful too, in its dark, luxuriant way.

Garden in a Small Town in Oklahoma

The brilliant orange lantana is
still dense in late October, protection
for sparrows, who attend the feeders made of gourds,
and do not care that they are garishly painted
or that one feeder looks like a tiny barn.
The pruned fruit trees are guyed with wires,
red plastic flowers placed amidst the hostas,
the castor bean plant shorn to stumps.
Yet the clumped cannas bloom on,
And roses, still lush, must be restrained with curtain rods.
Clumsy pruning has left gaps in the hedge.
And in the front yard, white ducks cut
with a jigsaw line up before the hollies.
No other yard is quite like it.
In there spring, there is no hydrangea bush
such an unearthly blue. No other place shows such
fierce attention—not the yards of those
who prefer the simplicity of grass and junipers,
or the yard of the iris lady, who loves only iris,
or that of the columned house
with its orderly shrubs and the little statue of a cherub.
Here everything is watched over, gussied up, loved, and,
if needed, sprayed, fertilized, supported, deadheaded,
pruned back hard.

Garden Speaker

The garden speaker from Georgia
is regaling the assemblage—
five hundred midwestern women
and a handful of men in chinos.
He's an odd duck indeed
with his soft accent, eccentric dress
(caftan, shawl, and silky skullcap,
like a rabbinical student gone to seed).
He shows slides of his private paradise:
dogs gamboling in the snow
about an ivy-covered cottage,
the spiral staircase made of tin,
the well-set tables, decked with fruit and flowers,
the faux Greek ruin in the back yard
with altars to the four seasons
(primrose, sunflower, grass, and holly).
He makes references to the gods, especially Dionysus,
who transformed the body of Ampelus
into a fruit-bearing vine;
thus, wine and festive occasions.

"Well," says the next speaker,
a trim man in a vest,
ready to show his slides of
companion plants that work
and those that don't,
"no myths here."

Mullein

My neighbor's garden has amazed me all summer long
though his garden is given over to oddities.
He does not believe in planting in drifts,
does not go in for flow.
None of that garden foreplay
with shorter plants leading to taller.
Rather than softening the foundation
with junipers or yews,
he picked bowling balls.
He cultivates specimens.
Ten types of phlox, thirty of iris.
He lets come what will.

Thus, the mullein by the curb.
By June it rose high above grass and concrete,
shaped like a Saguaro cactus
and looking every bit as prickly
with its furry leaves,
its extended spike, poking at the sky,
and now in this dry September,
burned to a stiff, brown crisp.

The Dismal Garden

By the side of Sorrowful Lake,
in a courtyard of a decaying chateau,
is a garden long gone to ruin.
The wind moans—when it doesn't sigh:
so sad, so sad, so sad.
The rain drips, drips all day long,
and vine-covered trees hide the sun.
Beautiful roses bloomed, but they too passed
though the gardener tied up their heads with strings.
The plastic tulips that took their place
gave up the ghost long ago.
No one sits on the cold stone bench,
regarding the statue of The Dolorous One,
with her heavenward gaze
and her prayerful hands
covered with mold and moss,
and the ring of toadstools about her feet.
So sad, so sad, so sad.

In the Garden with Thousands of Little Friends

> *The butterflies and bees*
> *Make a lovely little breeze,*
> *And the rabbits stand around and hold the lights.*
>   -Rose Fyleman

First to arrive, the flirtatious cabbage loopers,
fluttering here and there, depositing eggs,
which grow into big, strapping larvae.
I used to play games with the moths.
They'd flutter by, and I would try to net them
though I might have looked a little loopy.

When in June, the squash began to wilt,
I parted the stems and leaves, and there they were,
the subtle, swift squash bugs, so deft
and skittery, they remind me of
our kitchen companions, the roaches.

And let's give it up for the harlequin beetles.
Though some may call them stink bugs,
note their interesting red and black pattern
like the dress of their namesake.
Always constant, bless their hearts,
they went right to work on the kale, cauliflower,
collards, and cabbage. They prefer vegetables
that begin with a hard *C* sound, yet they
never miss my arugula. "Naughty, naughty,"
I said and pulled it before they spoiled their appetites.

The grasshoppers have just shown up.
Now they are little and cute, but soon
they'll be big and take a stance
at the top of a stalk. And when you pass,
they'll hop on and prickle your bare shoulder,
a little prank they like to play.

This year I've missed the yellow jackets in the pipe,
Missed their striking colors and pizzzzzzazzzzzz,
but not their sting. Too much of a good thing.

I almost forgot the wee ones—
the aphids, white flies, and the almost invisible spider mites.
Some say mites suck. True enough,
and if you listen very closely,
you'll hear the sound of thousands
of tiny straws at work. The plants may gasp and wilt
but the mites get merry on tomato bisque.

Finally, what's an evening without mosquitoes?
They don't give a fig for vegetables,
but how they love the week-old water in the birdbath,
though not as much as they love me.
In the garden one never is at a loss for friends.

Me, Traveler

Foreigners have such a je ne sai quoi.

Backdrop

The vacationers, who have settled themselves nicely
in navy and white striped canvas chairs,
along an S-curve facing the pool,
contrast pleasantly as bright dabs of color:
    the brown-skinned girl in yellow swimsuit,
    the pot-bellied man in red trunks,
    the woman in purple sarong taking a photo.
And nature has been edited to enhance the effect of
    the variegated turquoise waters in the sea,
    the white, seaweed-free sand,
    the aquamarine pools,
    the scatterings of palm trees,
    the rock reef beefed up into a barrier.
And out in the harbor a colossal cruise ship sounds a bass note
to accompany
    percussive human voices,
    the tinkling of calypso,
    the oboeing of the gulls,
    the slap-dash, slap-dash of waves,
        under a warm sun
        with a cool breeze.
The stage is set.

Foreigners Have Such a *Je Ne Sais Quoi*

I am mainly thinking of Central Europeans,
Hungarians particularly, with their hunter's stew,
paprikas, cherry syrups, *szaloncukor**
their strange, beautiful capital split by a river.
They resemble their czardas,
which mix heaviness and lightness,
are like playful bears, but intelligent,
like smiling cats, considering when to pounce.
Hungarians seem always to be playing chess
with you. Their eyes light up in sympathy
and amusement when you pronounce
igen, nem, kérem, közönöm.**
(*Our language is easy,* they joke; *that's why
Hungarians are such good readers.*)
What can one make of them?
In the rain, crossing the Liberty Bridge,
I pause to take a picture of the Liberation Monument***
on the Buda side, while on foot women
in head scarves and leather coats
and men with dark faces, smoking cigarettes,
give me passing glances while I stand pale and stolid
in my all-weather coat, handbag dangling,
an American smile on my lips.

---

*Christmas candy
***yes, no, please, thank you*
****a monument in Budapest erected in 1947 to commemorate the
Soviet liberation of the city from Nazi occupation.*

Visiting My Brother in Hungary, 1978

My brother has cleaned his apartment.
He offers coffee, tea, and something
red, syrupy, and authentic,
supermarket Hungarian cookies.
His hand-washed socks are coupled
and drying on the radiator.
(My friends look askance
whenever he's out of the room.)
Soon he shows us our schedule for
visits to Janos and Karoly and
the lady he says is
his Hungarian mother,
and later a day at a cottage
where workers take their vacations
and grow their own vegetables.
Tonight, we dine at a local place
on paprikaed pork with noodles,
potatoes heavy with cream.
But first some hints on things
that anger Hungarian cops,
which mainly boil down to pot.
My friends smile weakly.
Unfortunately, he's the host,
and they're trapped by the coffee and sweets,
and though their smiles
foreshadow rebellion,
for now it looks like they're caught
in my brother's version
of People to People
like it or not.

Foreign Tongues

How wonderful to hear them
as one is lying on a beach somewhere
or walking through some metro station,
foreign vocalizations,
the *ts, ts* like a little bug,
the *sh*, the *ch* that sounds like
a clearing of the throat,
strange vibrations, aspirations.
You need not understand a word.
It's better if you don't
though you might pick up
a *si* or *nyet* or *nem*.
But what is being approved or disapproved
you couldn't tell for the life of you,
so you need not respond at all
except to decide if you like sounds sibilant
or plosive. Do you mind the guttural?
Find appealing the rolling sound
of the subway conductor:
Következő állomas, Deák Tér?
You might be lulled and might forget
the sound does indicate a place—
it's on the map above your head—
must tell yourself, yes, yes,
get up, get off.

*Next station, Deák Square

With My Heavy-Drinking Friends in Europe

We had wine—in restaurants and on riverbanks,
in the hotels and on a train. No one was a teetotaler.
Once, when we were being loud and silly,
Shirley fretted we'd be thrown off the train,
which caused a fuss with Jean, our trip planner,
who angrily handed over the reservation-making to me.
That was in France, en route to Strasbourg.
We wound up in an old hotel where the floor buckled,
and Shirley worried the other guests were criminals.

On another trip through France, we mingled
with the crowd before a parade of cyclists. Everyone,
including us, wore yellow caps. Tipsy, we drove our little car
into the parade and waved flags and cheered
until officials kicked us out.

On the Rome trip, Mimi flirted with the waiters,
grew angry over some slight and argued loudly.
She was very drunk. I was by then
very middle-aged, and she embarrassed me.

We drove foreign cars everywhere.
In England, as the Seven Stone Wenches,
we took turns driving a van on the left side,
down narrow streets.
Pam, practicing her gear-shifting,
drove the van into the ocean.
In iron-curtain Czechoslovakia,
a friend rolled the car over a policeman's foot.

He railed at her in Czech. "Try your German,"
I said. She only smiled. He waved us off.

We traveled without reservations, stayed in B and B's.
My friends smoked a blue streak, smoked when it rained,
and the windows were sealed, at meals, espresso breaks,
and in between, had wine, beer, and harder stuff at dinner,
sometimes aperitifs or after-dinner brandies.
There were laughs and toasts and cigarette fogs.
Almost everyone is gone.

Out for a Walk

One summer I walked in Budapest
up and down Gellért Hill and Castle Hill,
along the Danube embankment,
across the river via the Liberty Bridge,
staring up at statues, monuments,
looking across at Pest, and the massive
buildings of the Hapsburgs
or down the rushing river with its pleasure ships,
past the tourist shops of Vaci Utca,
selling embroidered blouses,
paprika with wooden spoons, patterned rugs,
from Calvin Square to Heroes Square.

Many summers I've walked in Eufaula, Oklahoma,
past pecan trees full of webworm balloons,
black cows beneath trees, beside ponds,
across Business 69 aka Main Street,
before me Lake Eufaula, the "gentle giant"
where I've seen herons dipping beaks into muddy water,
walked past Braum's and craft shops
selling wrought iron, candles, kachina dolls, wind catchers,
and everywhere in this small town
American flags or yard signs
asserting American pride of place.

Catlike Me

The black cat, c'est moi.

Willy Nilly

> "When they aren't hunched like refugees on windowsills
> or scattered willy-nilly like cats, houseplants can transform a room."
>
> -Susan Heeger in *Martha Stewart Living*

I admit to having houseplants
scattered like cats,
and cats like houseplants,
all sunning themselves,
playing the part
of refugees on windowsills,
and recently a young cat
has planted himself willy-nilly
at our house, where he daily
launches himself upon his elders,
and fur flies like pollen,
and green leaves scatter,
so any human refugee,
standing outside,
peering over the wall
past the sunny window
during a fracas
as mites, mealy bugs, and fleas
swirl and scatter,
couldn't tell a cat from a cactus,
a paradise palm from a Persian,
a spider plant from the Siamese,
a bobtail from the American bonsai.

The Black Cat

Sometimes it's the neurotic black cat I feel for,
the pet most governed by moods.
The dog is adoring and docile.
He approaches us, tail wagging,
wants in, wants out, happy
at play or asleep, his tail twitching
in time to the usual doggy dreams.
And the new cat is a textbook study
in healthy emotional states—
curious, adaptive, persistent,
affectionate but independent,
never shocked by quarreling,
never whining, always asking openly,
never revengeful of the dog's clumsy play.
But the black one, the one unwanted
in childhood, though occasionally happy,
even blissful, is oftentimes sullen,
hissing, biting, refusing to eat,
terrified of strangers and most of the family,
always stalking off in a huff,
disdainful of cajolery but pissed without it,
with her ears flattened, her back arched,
her nose continually out of joint.
Yet, as Flaubert came close to saying,
"The black cat—*C'est moi.*"

Snow Scene with Cats

While all is silent and white flakes descend,
the cats and I are in the dining room.
The gray lounges on a canvas bag.
I stop writing, stare out the window.
The black also watches the white drift down.
The gray sky must have coaxed this sleepy pause.
The gray cat feels dull; the black, slightly curious.
She wonders why
the birds have left the feeder,
but isn't bothered. This is a time
for solemnity, not analysis.
We all hear something vaguely whining,
something that says be at ease,
take your leisure, twitch your paws,
run your fingers lightly over the keyboard.
Why try to rouse yourself?
It's black and gray and white outdoors.
If God spoke, he would sound like Edward R. Murrow.

The House Cat Vents

I am the one they call
Life-Is-Troubling-But-I-Manage-To-Entertain-Myself.
They refer to my cohort as *The Neurotic* or *The Easily Irritated*.
It's true. She's a moody creature, bites without provocation.
Sometimes I sympathize. They think a few bites of Fancy Feast,
a few pats, a few passes of the scratchy thing across our fur
will do. One spends one's days resting and roaming
throughout the house when one so badly wants a glimpse of life.
In short, one wants the back yard and front, I admit it.
Outside there are birds, very interesting creatures, though rather
flighty, and other cats, and occasionally, sad to say, dogs,
whose presence puts a damper on things, yet gives life meaning
since, it is rumored, some deal in death.
But outside one can see close up
more than the occasional housefly,
the woman coming and going with the laundry,
the man listening to the newscaster ironically named Wolf
when we could be watching *Amazing Videos of Cats*.
And the dog (not a credible dog, but an ungainly imitation),
lies splayed on the carpet like an Alpaca rug.
One wants to inflict serious damage on such a dog,
rake him and the legs of the people with sharp claws.
Instead one settles for the furniture and the oriental rug,
which drives them batty since they are supposed to be humane.
What they really want to do is fling us across the room and shout,
"Let's get it on!" In fact, they're every bit as bored
but without our heightened awareness.
Sartre had it right. No exit here.
I think Sartre was a cat in a former life.

Cat People

> "Forty-six percent of those polled thought people with four to six cats were likely to become hoarders."
>
> -Internet post for *Paw Nation*

A yellow cat is at the door.
Should they let it in? And if they did,
would they cross some sort of border?
Inside, three cats already patrol the house,
jump onto the kitchen counter,
come and go and speak not of Michelangelo
but of cat irritations and vexations,
making cat demands, speaking in cat tongues.
At night, their fur (matted, rough, or sleek)
sticks to the couple, and the couple breathe it in.
The house grows hairy.
Summer segues into fall, and they let in
Front Door Kitty. In winter they harbor
a pretty calico in their garage, who in April
has a little fling before they get her fixed.
And now there are nine. "What the hell,"
say the couple and take the plunge,
joining the legion of crazy cat people.
A gray and white short hair finds its way inside
and a sad old Persian. A skittery Siamese
sneaks in through an open window.
And so it goes. Friends drop away,
and soon the house becomes
"the house with a hundred cats."
though there are only forty-eight.

Now they awake to yowling, scratching,
hissing. "Which one cried out?" they ask
themselves. "Petey Boy or Slim or Satin?"
People stare from windows as they
stand on deck, tossing cat food
to the moving carpet of cats below,
scattering food, scattering
bits and pieces of themselves.

Irascible, Irritable, Petty, Pissed-off Me

Everything irritates me.

At the All-Day Meeting

Everything irritates me:
the stuffy, windowless room,
the man with the toothpick in his mouth,
the leftover gourmet brownies on the table.
I have already had one, but I want another.
The half sandwich from my box lunch shriveling
    before my eyes.
Its dryness and predictability irritate me
as does the predictability of the whole box lunch:
the fruit cup, the turkey and ham sandwich,
the pasta salad thick with mayo, the peanut butter cookie,
the Diet Coke.
All these things are irritating beyond belief.
The good-hearted, red-haired chairman, who is presiding
    and taking minutes—
his generosity and good will are annoying,
and so is his son, who made the gourmet brownies. He is
    only thirteen and already a pastry chef in training,
but they are less annoying than the gray-haired woman
    who "talks turkey" to the man in charge of the budget.
That we are "in this together" irritates me
as do my own smiles and laughter
and the laughter of the woman with the pretty blonde hair
and the woman with the encyclopedic knowledge.
She hunches protectively over her laptop.
But neither are as irksome as the turkey-talking woman
    when she inquires about the brownies.

The twenty-two-point agenda is enormously irritating
and the camaraderie and "partnering"
and our budget in the red
and the need to cut costs
and being asked to donate half our mileage expenses to
    the red budget
and that some feel compelled to donate *all* their mileage,
and that our box lunches may be our next donations
(but not the pastries, which were donated by the thirteen-
    year old chef).
And when someone says we should bring our own lunches,
    I am irritated,
and someone already is,
and her bottle of mocha-flavored soy milk sits on the table
    and looks like sludge.
And the associate vice-president asks each of us to share
"the single most rewarding thing about the meeting."
And some say. "the partnering,"
And the woman who has cornered the brownies says,
    "recharging my batteries."
But when I say. "the desserts," people look askance.
And finally, the meeting starts to shut down,
and the chair asks who won't be on board next year,
and the woman with the brownies says she won't,
and someone literally twists her arm and says, "Oh, please,
    please stay."
And I say, "I won't. I won't be on board."
But no one twists my arm,
so I stare at the brownies,
whose owner glances my way before she boxes them up.

Cross Patch

Cross patch, draw the latch,
Sit by the fire and spin . . .
    -Mother Goose

It's a day when you want to
chew someone up
and spit them out.
If they're smart, people
won't try to get you on the phone
but will leave you alone
with your little bits of piecework,
your little bits of tit-for-tatting,
let you spin your small scheme
for getting what's due
as you settle into
your comfortable chair,
your scratched and bruised mood,
so you can look out on the day
with an evil eye.

Damn Cross

I have crossed over into the land of crossness.
I am tired and weary. I want to lay my burdens down—
just the burdens mind you.
I carry many crosses, tedious crosses.
The crosses of my hair, my teeth.
The crosses of my messy house, the laundry,
my cats, my dog, my aging husband,
my children, and grandchildren.

Someone recently lied to me again.
I wasn't surprised, not even disappointed.
Just cross. I fumed and fumed.
She said she had completed certain jobs,
but there they lay before me, shining
in the sun, so I grew cross.
I removed her from the category of embellisher
and placed her in the category of liar.
Eventually I returned her. But I sulked.

Sometimes acid reflux flares,
and I get crosser. Once I moaned for days,
like Olympia Dukakis in *Moonstruck*.
I love that moan. It expresses me.
It escapes like steam from a kettle,
an almost unconscious sound,
but I confess it's part of my act.
I suffer, it says. My life consists of petty sufferings.
Not agony, just endless tedium and pin pricks.

When my stomach churns up a little acid,
I like to look in the mirror and see
my face all pitiful and hangdog.
I'm smart enough not to come across that way
to just anyone. I save it mostly for my husband.
He doesn't buy it, but maybe sometimes he wonders.

Christmas Shopping

I am stuck in a line
with a cashier aptly named Amelia.
The women in front of me have questions
about all the numbers
on the tickets they hold up, which
Amelia must make sense of
and does so very patiently,
explaining to all good-naturedly
as she rings them up
while discoursing on percentages,
then leaves her position
to locate the manager
while we in line watch her departure
with sorrow.
Then the manager explains the policy
as Amelia indicates with index
finger how things transpire on
the register, proving that
all that should be counted is, and things
that shouldn't be, aren't.

Oh, Amelia, dear girl,
even though it's Christmas,
for a moment I hate you,
hate your sweet, round face,
your heavy eyelids, and pale lips,
your eagerness to explore all

the ins and outs of shopping
with the white-haired mother,
whom I'll call Sally,
and the straw-blonde daughter,
whom I'll call Terri.
I hate them too, their register
watching, their very particular
questions. I even hate
the woman in the jaunty cap,
who skips out to a better line,
leaving me with Amelia,
Sally, and Terry, who gather
up all their gift receipts,
fold them carefully and say,
"So sorry this took so long,"
and leave. "Have a merry Christmas,"
Amelia tells me. "The same to you,"
I say, my smile tight and thin,
so mealy-mouthed, I hate myself.
A Christmas blessing though.
My face is hot, but the day is cold,
and the walk to the car—
thank you, Jesus—is long.

Tweak

Everywhere people are tweaking things,
not just stray hairs from an eyebrow
but statistics, conclusions, sentences, sentiments,
punch lines, recollections, images,
the base and treble on the stereo,
the reading on the bathroom scale
(by moving the scale or exhaling),
lyrics, agendas, apologies, farewells:
Goodbye, no I mean *adios*.
No, I mean *auf Weiderschen*.
Even prayers:
God, let him love me.
On second thought, make that *adore*.
Not content with fine-tuning,
tweakers prefer twisting and plucking,
pricking out X, teasing Y into place.
Their model, the dentist,
who worries a tooth with
a cold, metal pick
until the patient, gripping
the arms of the chair, cries,
"For God's sake, just pull it!"
"Of course," he says.
"I mean to do exactly that.
But first I need to probe.
Just a bit."

Transcendent Me

After dark, we are Buddhists together.

Without Fear of Plummeting

I think I could turn and live with animals.
  -Walt Whitman

I might turn and live with animals
if they would let me into their little shelters,
if I could manage to follow them up and down hills,
through brush over fallen limbs,
or if I could follow through the air,
perch on top of a building or wire
without fear of plummeting,
or wade offshore in cold water all year,
with no fear of freezing, no holding back,
like the heron plunging headfirst into water
or swimming in a cold stream with no
lengthy testing of temperatures,
no dipping of toes in the water.
Or like the cats who sit on the deck rail,
level with the tree branches, looking over
the back yard, curious or watchful
or zenlike, eyes wide, yet zoned out.
Or lazing in the sun, content.
Or like the dog, patiently scratching.
Or the squirrels playing, circling the tree trunk,
unaware of death swooping down from above.

Contemplatives

After returning to our "real home,"
we are welcomed back by three cats,
two quite old, one plagued by diabetes
and kidney disease, doing okay
but his eyes water, and his hair sticks out
in separate mats, which turn him into a big hedgehog.

He nestles in my lap, head on the chair's arm.
A year ago, he quit grooming himself, so I groom him,
as a mother monkey picks nits from her young,
tediously separating the fur on his forehead,
teasing bits of ick and hair from his head.
When I'm done, he has a little mohawk, looks spiff.
If he weren't fixed, he'd receive invitations.

Ancient history. He's become a contemplative.
He lies in the sun and focuses on his breathing.
After dark, we become Buddhists together, gazing
with half-shut eyes at the falling snow.
My eyes are sleepy; his, rheumy.
The world outside is pleasantly blurry.

MRI

While the magnets are bouncing off
my sore knee in its little plastic cradle,
and with my ear plugs in place for protection,
the machine and I are imaging.
Now the machine's voice thrums like a Buddhist monk,
saying *relax, focus on your breathing.*
But my mind is wandering, thinking daffodils, for instance,
because of a certain yellow light in the room.
Or, because of the thing's tunnel shape,
I'm thinking spring, rebirth,
even out of plastic wombs.
And now a drilling sound resonates with images:
a bird is pecking on flagstones,
a man is drilling with a little jackhammer,
a riveter is shooting rivets,
and in a yellow land and sky,
a gunner is firing an automatic rifle
aimlessly at the horizon, across the desert
for the pure monotony of it,
firing as if through cotton. At nothing.

Recycled

A shredded draft of my ms
is in the compost, mingling with "leaves of grass,"
weeds, and true leaves, as from oak and maple.
The pieces, bits of a chapter wherein the lovers screwed,
are undergoing earthly changes
as fungi, microbes, and pill bugs begin their tedious work.
Perhaps a *b* that was the start of a *breast*
that belonged to a character named Marge
and a *p* that was part of the hero's . . .
Well, there's no need to dwell on what it *was*
because next spring, oh glorious spring,
it will nourish plants, who would otherwise
grow into scrawny, unsexy things
without a hope of drawing the least little bee.

Duo

A matching pair of old ladies
is puttering around in adjacent yards
in the buttery light of early morning,
neither aware of the other, but
observed by some third party,
who notes their matching gray hair,
the curvature of their spines,
which has converted them into *C's,*
their similar canes, which they use
to poke about in the dirt—
so many resemblances the observer
might extrapolate that at this hour
X number of equivalent old ladies
are puttering about
in similar plots all over town.
That would be an oversimplification.
Observe them more closely.
One is now righting herself.
The other, bent over,
has become an upside-down *U*
just as above them the green leaves
of the fluttering apple tree
are glossy or matte, moving or still,
depending on minute variations
in the light and in the breeze
passing through the scene.

It Was Green

> *. . . I was young and easy under the apple boughs,*
> *happy as the grass was green.*
> -Dylan Thomas

It was amazingly green south down I-35,
lush in the undulating Flint Hills,
bright green background for
jetblack cattle, set perfectly in place.

Green all the way to Stillwater:
green grass, green fields, green trees,
moss-green ponds and roadside ditches,
brimming with rainwater, spring having overflowed

into summer. Then, children at the reunion,
green and easy, adults green with envy,
suburban green lawns, flawless,
splashed with red, white, pink crape myrtles.

But, heading back, for a moment
gray inside the highway Hardee's,
Everyone gray-faced from travel and heat.
Gray wall, gray tile, steel-gray fixtures.

Then back on the road, headed home—
green again, with late afternoon gold splotches,
blue skies with fathappy clouds,
the a.c. on, and everything,
everything green and humming.

The Little Creek

It was a now and then, off and on little creek
that ran in its little valley at the bottom of the street.
It dried up in summer, but in wet weather rose
high enough to flood a basement.
In spring it drew us, and we followed it into the woods,
especially when the sweet Williams and the May apples blossomed.
Once, hoping to catch a water bug, we scooped
its muddy waters into a clear jar and watched the water
separate into muck below and clear brown above.
And surprise! we found a round, brown water boatman,
who swam around just for us, then hid in the muck.
The next day we released him and wondered
if he and his fellow boatmen followed
the meandering creek south through the woods
into someone else's bigger creek,
and on and on into the Kaw, the Missouri
and the big wide waters of the world.

Pat Lawson has lived in the Kansas City area all her life and now lives in Kansas City, Kansas. She is a retired English instructor (KCKCC), an avid gardener, and vice president of her neighborhood group. She volunteers on the Riverfront Readings Committee and the Writers Place Program Committee. Her poetry and prose have appeared in many journals and magazines. *Why We Love Our Cats and Dogs* (with the late Philip Miller and published by Unholy Day Press) contains her stories and poems. A collection of stories, *Odd Ducks*, was published in October 2020 by BkMk Press.

www.ingramcontent.com/pod-product-compliance
Lightning Source LLC
Chambersburg PA
CBHW022008120526
44592CB00034B/739